Wildflowers
of the **Pacific Northwest**

T0166291

Adventure Quick Guides

YOUR WAY TO EASILY IDENTIFY WILDFLOWERS

Adventure Quick Guides

This Pacific Northwest Quick Guide highlights 248 of the showiest and most common wildflowers seen in Washington, Oregon, and Idaho, as well as a number of significant rare and endangered species. From the towering forest trees to the smallest meadow wildflowers, each plant species is adapted to a narrow set of growing conditions, and the Pacific Northwest and Idaho have an incredibly diverse range of habitats. They range from the Pacific shore in the west, across the forested Coastal Range, through the interior valleys, up the rain-drenched western slopes of the Cascades, over the alpine meadows and glaciated peaks, down the dry eastern slopes and foothills to the arid, cold sagebrush deserts of eastern Oregon and Washington, then into the Basin and Range, Badlands and Northern Rockies of Idaho. This Quick Guide introduces you to the astounding variety of wildflowers that cover every niche of this dynamic corner of the continent.

GEORGE MILLER

Longtime botanist and nature photographer George Miller has explored the West for 30 years and has published in books, magazines, and newspapers. He's written nine guidebooks to plants and animals of the Southwest, including the best-selling *Landscaping with Native Plants of Southern California*. He's also written Quick Guides to wildflowers of Southern California, Northern California, Colorado, and Texas, as well as five smartphone wildflower guides.

Cover and book design by Lora Westberg
Edited by Brett Ortler

Cover image: Columbia Lily by George Miller
All images copyrighted
All images by George Miller unless otherwise noted

John Brew: Calochortus macrocarpus; **Cbaile 19, Own work, Creative Commons CC0 1.0 Universal Public Domain Dedication:** Viola glabella; **maras~commonwiki, Public Domain:** Trillium ovatum; **Forest Service Northern Region from Missoula, MT, Public Domain:** Cypripedium montanum; **Ben Salzberg:** Darlingtonia california (main image); **US Forest Service-Pacific Northwest Region, Public Domain:** Lysichiton americanus

10 9 8 7 6 5 4 3

Wildflowers of the Pacific Northwest

Copyright © 2019 by George Miller
Published by Adventure Publications, an imprint of AdventureKEEN
310 Garfield Street South, Cambridge, Minnesota 55008
(800) 678-7006
www.adventurepublications.net
All rights reserved
Printed in China
ISBN 978-1-59193-827-9 (pbk.)

KEY

- Wildflowers are sorted into four groups by color and organized within groups from smaller to larger blooms.
- Leaf attachment icons are shown next to each wildflower.
- Descriptions include important facts such as cluster shape, number of petals, or center color to help you quickly identify the species. Size information is sometimes included as well.

LEAF ATTACHMENT

Wildflower leaves attach to stems in different ways. The leaf icons next to the flowers show alternate, opposite, whorled, perfoliate, clasping, and basal attachments. Some wildflower plants have two or more types of leaf attachments.

 ALTERNATE leaves attach in an alternating pattern.

 OPPOSITE leaves attach directly opposite each other.

 BASAL leaves originate at the base of the plant and are usually grouped in pairs or in a rosette.

 PERFOLIATE leaves are stalkless and have a leaf base that completely surrounds the main stem.

 CLASPING leaves have no stalk, and the base partly surrounds the main stem.

 WHORLED leaves have three or more leaves that attach around the stem at the same point.

 CLUSTERED leaves originate from the same point on the stem.

 SPINES are leaves that take the form of sharp spines.

PARTS OF A FLOWER

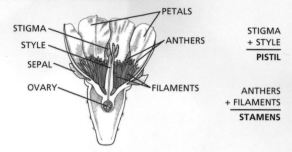

OCEANS, MOUNTAINS, DESERTS

The Pacific Northwest contains about a dozen widely different ecological regions. For an idea of just how different they are: 122 inches of rain fall annually along the northern coast of Washington; the desert plateaus east of the Cascades receive a scant 8 inches a year. And each ecological region harbors a distinct community of plant life. Pacific currents bathe the shoreline and temperate Coastal Range with moisture-laden clouds that nourish forests with the highest biomass per acre on the planet. Fertile intermountain valleys give way to the moist slopes and snow-capped peaks of the Cascades, which spawn the most glaciers in the Lower 48. The wall of mountains blocks the Pacific rain flow to create a rain shadow across the eastern plateaus. Sagebrush and grasses dominate the cold, treeless desert.

From early spring through fall, you can find an abundance of wildflowers blooming somewhere in the PNW. After a winter of dormancy, wildflowers along the coast from Seattle to southern Oregon greet spring rains. As the valleys and west-slope forests warm, perennial flowers re-emerge and annuals germinate. Wildflowers along the east-slope forests follow, and if weather patterns are generous, desert brushlands join with a riotous spring bloom. Then as the grand finale, late-summer snow melt in the Cascades and Northern Rockies triggers the alpine meadows to explode with one of the most spectacular wildflower pageants on the planet. This Quick Guide will help you name the beautiful wildflowers you discover across the Pacific Northwest and Idaho.

Artemisia ludoviciana

Silver Wormwood

Stems gray-woolly, clumping, 12–40 inches; spike of small, bell-shaped flowers; aromatic leaves

Amsinckia intermedia

Common Fiddleneck

Stem 1–2 feet, bristly hairs; small, tubular orange-yellow flowers in a coiled spike; narrow leaves

Berberis aquifolium

Oregon Grape

Evergreen shrub; clusters of small, yellow flowers; leaflets lined with prickles; blue berries; forests

Berberis repens

Trailing Oregon Grape

Groundcover; clusters of small, yellow flowers; leaflets lined with prickles; blue berries; forests

Eriogonum umbellatum

Sulphur Flower Buckwheat

Mat-forming; flower stem with a leaf-like whorl; flowers in spherical clusters; oval leaves

Foeniculum vulgare

Sweet Fennel

Clumps to 6 feet tall; tiny flowers in flat-topped clusters; hair-like leaves; roadside weed

Pterospora andromedea

no leaves

Woodland Pinedrops

Erect reddish, leafless stem; spike of tiny, urn-shaped flowers; parasitic on conifer roots

Tribulus terrestris

Goathead

Mat-forming stems to 3 feet wide; 5 petals; fruit a thorny nutlet; elliptic leaflets; weedy

Whitestem Blazing Star

Stem to 1 foot; oval petals; club-shaped, hairy capsule; lobed, Velcro-like leaves; widespread

Birdsfoot Trefoil

Stems 1–2 feet; pea-like flowers in round clusters on a leafless stalk; 5 oval leaflets; weedy

Yellow Sweet-Clover

Stems 20–60 inches; spike of tubular, slightly drooping flowers; 3 oval, toothed leaflets; weedy

Golden Currant

Shrub 3–9 feet, thornless; clustered flowers, 5 narrow petals; orange to red berry; 3-lobed leaf

Western Goldenrod

Stem 1–5 feet, hairless; large pyramidal array of small flowers; lance-shaped, toothed leaves

Mountain Goldenrod

Hairless stem to 30 inches; flower cluster round to slender; lance-shaped leaves; coast to alpine

Broom Snakeweed

Rounded, 1–3 feet tall; dense flower clusters, 3–5 tiny rays; thread-like leaves; brushlands

Smooth Sumac

Small tree; tiny, yellowish-green flowers in a dense cluster; fruit a red berry; lance-shaped leaflets

Streptopus amplexifolius

Clasping Twisted Stalk
Stems 2–3 feet; bell-shaped, yellow-green flowers dangle on twisted stalk; fruit a red berry; oval leaves

Tanacetum bipinnatum

Dune Tansy
Stem 4–12 inches; button-like flower head; disk florets only, no rays; fern-like, woolly leaves; coastal

Abronia latifolia

Yellow Sand-Verbena
Prostrate stems on beaches; spherical clusters of trumpet-shaped flowers; thick, oval leaves

Purshia tridentata

Bitterbrush
Shrub 3–7 feet; 5 rounded petals; wedge-shaped, 3-lobed leaves, in bundles; forests

Sedum lanceolatum

Lanceleaf Stonecrop
Stem 1–7 inches; star-shaped flowers; green to red, lance-shaped, succulent leaves; forests

Sedum oreganum

Pacific Stonecrop
Stem 3–6 inches; pointed petals; green to red, crowded, oval, succulent leaves; coast to forest

Ericameria nauseosa

Rabbitbrush
Shrub to 6 feet; dense clusters of tiny, tubular flowers; narrow, gray/green leaves; brushlands

Agoseris aurantiaca

Orange False-Dandelion
Stem 4–24 inches; narrow, toothed rays; no disk flowers; elliptic or lobed leaves; milky sap; forests

Common Dandelion

Stem 2–15 inches; many ray florets, tips toothed; fruit a feathery puff-ball; lobed leaves; weedy

Yellow Salsify

Stem 12–30 inches; bracts longer than rays; fruit a feathery puff-ball; grass-like leaves; weedy

Wallflower

Stems 2–4 feet; spherical flower clusters, yellow or red-orange petals; pods parallel to stems

Hairy Cat's-Ear

Stem to 30 inches; many notched ray florets, reddish on backside; hairy, lobed leaves; weedy

Large-leaf Avens

Stems 8–40 inches; petals don't overlap, rounded to notched tips; toothed leaflets; moist soils

Stinking Willie

Stems leafy, 2–4 feet; clustered flower heads; elliptic rays; deeply lobed, fernlike leaves; weedy

Woolly Groundsel

Stems 4–12 inches, all foliage woolly-white; clustered flower heads, 8–13 rays; woolly basal leaves; sagebrush to forests

Rocky Mountain Groundsel

Stems 4–25 inches; clustered flowers; long-stemmed, oval, usually hairless basal leaves; forests

Yellow to Orange

Senecio integerrimus

Western Groundsel
Hairy stems 8–30 inches; clustered flowers, 8 rays; lance-shaped leaves; sage to forests

Senecio triangularis

Arrowleaf Groundsel
Stems to 5 feet; flower heads have 8 rays, yellow disk; triangular, toothed leaves; moist soils

Leontodon saxatilis

Hawkbit
Leafless stems to 12 inches; buds nod; flower head with 20–30 notched rays; naturalized

Orthocarpus luteus

Yellow Owl's Clover
Hairy, often reddish stems, 4–16 inches; tubular flowers have hooded tip; narrow leaves; forests

Lupinus arboreus

Yellow Bush Lupine
Shrub to 6 feet; spikes of yellow flowers; hairy pod; leaf with 5–20 radiating leaflets; coastal

Thermopsis montana

Mountain Golden Pea
Stems 1–2.5 feet; spikes of golden, pea-like flowers; leaves with 3 elliptic leaflets; forests

Pedicularis bracteosa

Fern-leaf Lousewort
Stems 1–3 feet; flowers yellow to purple-tinted, hood covers lower lip; fernlike leaves; forests

Lonicera involucrata

Twinberry
Shrub; tubular, yellow to orangish paired flowers; paired fruit; black berries; oval leaves; forests

Yellow Monkeyflower

Stems 2–3 feet; flower lower lobe bearded with red spots; rounded leaves; in wet areas

Golden Corydalis

Stems 8–14 inches; flowers tubular with horizontal spur; fernlike leaves; sage to forests

Common Toadflax

Stems 1–3 feet; flowers creamy-yellow; an orange lip, slender spur points downward; weedy

Mullein

Stems to 6 feet tall; spike of small yellow flowers; large, fuzzy basal leaves; roadside weed

Moth Mullein

Stems to 3 feet; yellow or white flowers with purple centers; toothed leaves; roadside weed

Shrubby Cinquefoil

Shrub to 3 feet; 5 oval petals, showy stamens; narrow, pointed, crowded leaflets; forests

Silverweed Cinquefoil

Prostrate, spreading red stems; 5-petaled flowers; 10–20 toothed leaflets spread along midrib

Slender Cinquefoil

Stems 8–30 inches tall; 5-petaled flowers; 5–7 toothed leaflets radiate from stem; widespread

Potentilla flabellifolia

Fan-leaf Cinquefoil
Stem 6–12 inches; cup-shaped flowers, many stamens; 3 hairless, toothed leaflets; mountains

Drymocallis glandulosa

Sticky Cinquefoil
Stems 6–30 inches; 5 yellow to cream petals; leaves with 1–4 paired leaflets; coast to forests

Ranunculus alismifolius

Water Plantain Buttercup
Stems 6–28 inches; 5–12 rounded petals; lance-shaped to elliptic leaves; moist soils

Viola glabella

Smooth Yellow Violet
Stem 1–12 inches; 3 lined lower petals; side petals bearded; heart-shaped leaves; moist soils

Heterotheca villosa

Hairy Goldenaster
Stems hairy, clump-forming, 6–30 inches; 10–20 yellow rays; oblong, hairy leaves; brushlands

Agoseris grandiflora

Giant Dandelion
Stems to 2 feet; ray florets only, tipped with tiny teeth; lobed leaves; milky sap; widespread

Hulsea nana

Dwarf Hulsea
Mat-forming, densely hairy; stem 4–6 inches; 12–30 notched rays; oblong lobed leaves; alpine

Hypericum scouleri

Western St. John's Wort
Stems 1–2 feet; clustered flowers; black dots line petals; oval, black-dotted leaves; moist forests

Avalanche Lily

Erythronium grandiflorum

Leafless stems; nodding yellow
flowers, petals curl backwards;
lance-shaped leaves; mountains

Common Madia

Madia elegans

Stems to 3 feet; 5–22 yellow
rays often with a maroon base;
narrow, hairy leaves; forests

Columbia Coreopsis

Coreopsis tinctoria

Stem 1–3 feet; rays yellow-orange
usually with a red-brown base;
narrow, lobed leaves; meadows

Hairy Gumweed

Grindelia hirsutula

Stems 1–2 feet; flower heads
resinous, sticky; 15–60 rays;
toothed leaves; coast to forests

Hairy Evening Primrose

Oenothera villosa

Stems 3–6 feet; rounded,
notched petals fade to orange;
lance-shaped leaves; moist forests

Heartleaf Arnica

Arnica cordifolia

Stem to 2 feet; lance to heart-
shaped; short-stalked leaves
with shallow teeth; meadows

Hairy Arnica

Arnica mollis

Stems 6–24 inches, hairy; rough,
lance-shaped leaves are not
stalked, teeth irregular; meadows

Broad-leaf Arnica

Arnica latifolia

Stems 4–20 inches; disk yellow
with white hairs; lance-shaped to
oval toothed leaves; meadows

Eriophyllum lanatum

Oregon Sunshine

Stems woolly, 4–40 inches; 5–13 yellow rays; yellow disk; leaves linear to lobed; forests

Eschscholzia californica

California Poppy

Flowers blanket hillsides with 4 gold to orange petals; leaves with fern-like lobes; yellow sap

Mentzelia laevicaulis

Giant Blazing Star

Stem to 3 feet; 5 pointed petals, many stamens; sandpapery, wavy and lobed leaves; widespread

Opuntia polyacantha

Plains Prickly Pear

Clumps one pad high; dense spines; solid yellow or magenta flowers; fruit is a spiny, tan capsule

Balsamorhiza sagittata

Arrowleaf Balsamroot

Stems to 16 inches, one flower head each; triangular, basal leaves up 1 foot long; widespread

Helianthus annuus

Annual Sunflower

Single stems 2–8 feet, 20+ flowers; yellow rays, red-brown disk; hairy triangular leaves; dry sites

Lilium columbianum

Columbia Lily

Stems to 5 feet; petals curl back; orange with maroon spots, tips often reddish; dry soils

Lysichiton americanus

Skunk Cabbage

Spike of small flowers hooded by 3–8 inch yellow bract; oval leaves, 1–2 feet long; wet soils

Red to Pink

Western Snakeroot
Shrubby, 2 feet; clustered, pink to white, tubular flowers; triangular-oval toothed leaves; forests

Nodding Onion
Stem with nodding cluster of urn-shaped flowers; grass-like leaves; onion aroma; spring blooming

Geyer's Onion
Stem with erect cluster of urn-shaped flowers; grass-like leaves; onion aroma; summer blooming

Pinesap
Stems red or yellow, 4–12 inches; spike nodding in flower, erect in fruit; scale-like leaves; forests

Lesser Burdock
Stems to 9 feet tall; thistle-like flower head with pink florets; oval leaves, 12–24 inches long

Sea Thrift
Stem 6–18 inches; flowers tiny in dense ¾-inch diameter cluster; grasslike leaves; coastal

Coyote Mint
Up to 2 feet tall; round flower cluster; thread-like, pink, white, or lavender petals; oval, fragrant leaves; widespread

Showy Milkweed
Up to 4 feet tall; clusters of rose-pink flowers; seed pods covered with warty prickles; milky sap; coastal, meadows

Spreading Phlox

Mat-forming; pink, white, or pale blue flowers; narrow, pointed leaves; open forests

Moss Campion

Mat 1–3 inches tall; pink to lavender flowers, tips notched; stiff linear leaves; alpine

Pink Mountain-Heather

Shrubby; bell-shaped, pink to rose flowers clustered at stem tips; evergreen needle-like leaves

Twinflower

Stem to 4 inches; paired, nodding, bell-shaped, pale pink flowers; oval leaves; forests

King's Crown

Stems to 20 inches tall; flowers in flattish clusters; crowded, pointed, succulent leaves; mountains

Meadowsweet

Shrub to 3 feet; round clusters of rosy-pink flowers; oval-elliptic, toothed leaves; forests

Green Manzanita

Shrub; reddish bark; clustered, urn-shaped, pinkish-white flowers; oval shiny leaves; forests

Mountain Snowberry

Shrub; flowers tubular with small spreading lobes; oval, pointed, hairless leaves; forests

Red to Pink

Elephant's Head Lousewort

Stems to 30 inches; flowers resemble a tiny elephant head; fernlike leaves; wet meadows

Pink Honeysuckle

Sprawling vine; tubular flowers; pink, hairy, curled petals; red fruit; oval leaves with hairy edges

Henbit

Stems 2–14 inches; tubular, pink to purple flowers in whorls; rounded leaves; weedy

Pygmy Bitterroot

Ground-hugging stems; petals pink with darker stripes; long, narrow leaves; high meadows

Spotted Coralroot Orchid

Red or yellow, pencil-thin, often clustered stems; lower flower lip has red spots; forests

Striped Coralroot Orchid

Red or yellow, pencil-thin, often clustered stems; lower lip has red-purple stripes; forests

Western Coralroot

Red or yellow, pencil-thin, often clustered stems; lower lip has 2 red veins and a nubby spur; forests

Prairie Smoke, Old Man's Whiskers

Red stalks to 8 inches; 3 urn-shaped, nodding flowers; feathery seeds; sagebrush to forests

Dwarf Monkeyflower

Stems 4 inches; paired pink or yellow flowers; throat has yellow and red marks; elliptic leaves

Bleeding Heart

Stems to 18 inches; dangling, heart-shaped, pink flowers; lobed, fern-like leaves; forests

Coastal Hedgenettle

Stem 3–8 feet, square, hairy; tubular flowers in separated whorls; oval, pointed, hairy leaves

Red Clover

Stem 6–24 inches, hairy; sphere of small tubular flowers; 3 oval leaflets with a light slash

Monterey Centaury

Branching stems to 12 inches; 5 rounded petals, white throat; oblong leaves; forests, foothills

Red-flowering Currant

Thornless shrub; dangling clusters, of red, pink, white flowers; fruit blue-black; lobed leaves; forests

Mountain Gooseberry

Thorny shrub to 5 feet; petals red to pink, tips inrolled; orange-red, bristly fruit; hairy leaves with 3–5 lobes

Salmonberry

Thornless shrub; pinkish-red flowers; yellow to red berries; 3 toothed leaflets; forests

Canada Thistle

Noxious weed to 4 feet; flower has purple-tinged spines, tassel-like flowers; lobed, spiny leaves

Indian Thistle

Stem 2–8 feet; head hairy with spiny bracts, tassel-like flowers; leaves spiny; coast, mountains

Wavyleaf Thistle

Stem 2–8 feet tall; bracts spiny with a white ridge; tassel-like flowers; wavy-lobed, spiny leaves

Wavy-leaf Paintbrush

Stems sticky-hairy, 7–27 inches; red, hairy bracts; lance-shaped leaves, edges wavy; forests

Cobwebby Paintbrush

Long, hairy stem up to 12 inches; lobed dull red to yellow, bracts; linear, lobed leaves; mountains

Desert Paintbrush

Reddish, hairy stem up to 18 inches; red, lobed bracts; narrow leaves, edges curve inward

Wyoming Paintbrush

Hairless stem up to 3 feet; bracts red with narrow lobes; narrow leaves, edges roll inward; dry woodlands

Scarlet Paintbrush

Hairy stem up to 30 inches; red hairy bracts with narrow lobes; lance-shaped leaves; mountains

Chamerion angustifolium

Calypso bulbosa

Fireweed

Stems chest-high, forms dense stands; spikes of pink flowers; coast to mountain slopes

Fairy Slipper Orchid

Stem to 8 inches; spreading side petals and red-spotted lip; one oval leaf; forests

Epipactis gigantea

Ipomopsis aggregata

Giant Helleborine Orchid

Leafy stems to 3 feet; veined pink to orange flowers; lower petal wiggles in the breeze; streamsides

Skyrocket

Stems to 3 feet; trumpet-like flowers, 5 petals with white spots; threadlike leaves; forests

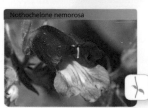
Nothochelone nemorosa

Penstemon rupicola

Woodland Penstemon

Stem 12–40 inches; tubular, red flower, throat often paler; lance-shaped, saw-toothed leaves

Rock Penstemon

Mat-forming, 4 inches tall; tubular, pink to rose flower; oval, finely toothed leaves; rocky slopes

Primula pauciflora

Rosa woodsii

Pretty Shooting Star

Stem to 2 feet; petals point upward, cone-shaped stamens downward; oval leaves; wet soils

Woods Rose

Thorny shrub, 3–9 feet; 5 petals; showy yellow stamens; 5–7 oval leaflets along midrib; forests

Convolvulus arvensis

Erigeron glaucus

Field Bindweed

Mat-forming vine spreads to
6 feet; pink to white flowers;
arrow-shaped leaves; weedy

Seaside Fleabane

Clump-forming to 1 foot tall;
pink, purple, or white rays;
yellow disk; oval leaves; coastal

Rhododendron macrophyllum

Aquilegia formosa

Pacific Rhododendron

Large shrub; dense clusters of bell-
shaped, pale pink to rose-purple
flowers; oblong leaves; forests

Western Columbine

Up to 2 feet tall; nodding flowers
have yellowish-tipped petals and
long, straight, red spurs; forests

Mimulus lewisii

Clarkia amoena

Lewis Monkeyflower

Stems 1–3 feet; pink to rose
flowers, spreading petals; oblong
leaves; mountains

Farewell to Spring

Stem 1–3 feet; 4 pale pink to red
petals with a red central spot;
linear leaves; coast to forests

Darlingtonia californica

Digitalis purpurea

California Pitcher Plant

Basal leaves pitcher-shaped,
mottled; flower stem 2–3 feet;
5 reddish-green, veined petals;
found in wetlands

Common Foxglove

Stems to 6 feet; one-sided spike;
nodding, tubular, flowers with
purple spots inside; lance-shaped
leaves; coastal to wet forests

White to Green

Bistorta bistortoides

Angelica lucida

Western Bistort
Up to 2 feet; oblong cluster of tiny white to pink flowers; lance-shaped leaves; moist soils

Sea-Watch
Stems 2–4 feet; small flowers in tight spherical clusters; leaves sheath stem, leaflets lobed; coastal

Cicuta douglasii

Conium maculatum

Water Hemlock
Stems to 6 feet; spherical clusters of tiny flowers; narrow toothed leaflets; wet soils; **deadly toxic**

Poison Hemlock
Purple-spotted stems to 10 feet; rounded flower clusters; parsley-like leaves; wet soils; **deadly toxic**

Daucus carota

Cornus sericea

Queen Anne's Lace
Up to 4 feet tall; umbrella-like cluster; tiny maroon flower in the center; parsley-like leaves; weedy

Red Osier Dogwood
Shrub, red stems; rounded flower cluster; fruit a white berry; triangular, veined leaves; forests

Achillea millefolium

Cardaria draba

Common Yarrow
Stems 1–3 feet tall; flat clusters of tiny white flowers; aromatic fernlike leaves; widespread

Hoary Cress
Stem 1–2 feet; clusters of small flowers; heart-shaped pods; lance-shaped leaves; weedy

White to Green

Comandra umbellata

Bastard Toadflax

Stems 3–20 inches; creamy to pinkish petals, anthers brown; narrow to elliptic leaves; weedy

Cistanthe umbellata

Pussytoes

Stem to 2 feet, erect or prostrate; spherical white or pink clusters; spatula-shaped leaves; mountains

Anaphalis margaritacea

Pearly Everlasting

Up to 3 feet; some flowers have yellow florets in the center; narrow leaves; coast to forests

Apocynum androsaemifolium

Spreading Dogbane

Branching to 3 feet tall; bell-shaped, slightly nodding flowers; broad, pointed leaves; forests

Aruncus dioicus

Bride's Feathers

Bushy, 2–7 feet tall; plume-like clusters of tiny flowers; serrated, pointed leaflets; forests

Asclepias fascicularis

Narrow-leaf Milkweed

Stems 2–3 feet; round clusters of creamy-pink flowers; narrow leaves; milky sap; moist soils

Maianthemum racemosum

False Lily of the Valley

Stem 12–36 inches; feathery plume; sword-like leaves with distinct parallel veins; forests

Maianthemum stellatum

Star Solomon's Seal

Stems 12–28 inches; one star-shaped flower per tiny branch; sword-like leaves; forests

White to Green

Eriogonum elatum

Tall Buckwheat
Stem 16–32 inches; spherical cluster of small flowers; hairy lance-shaped leaves; sage-shrub

Eriogonum microthecum

Great Basin Buckwheat
Bushy, 1–3 feet; white to pink flowers in flat-topped clusters; narrow leaves; brushlands

Eriogonum nudum

Naked Buckwheat
Stems 4–60 inches; spherical white to pink clusters; oblong leaves, woolly bottoms; forests

Eriogonum ovalifolium

Cushion Buckwheat
Mat-forming stems 2–4 inches tall; white to pink clusters; oval, hairy leaves; widespread

Eriogonum pyrolifolium

Alpine Buckwheat
Flower stem 2–4 inches; white spherical clusters aging to pink, dark anthers; elliptic, hairy leaves

Rumex crispus

Curly Dock
Stem 12–40 inches; cluster of greenish flowers; lance-shaped leaves, edges wrinkled; weedy

Gaultheria shallon

Salal
Coastal thicket-forming shrub to 6 feet; white to pink flowers; black fruit; oval, leathery leaves

Marah oregana

Coastal Manroot
Vine; bell-shaped, cream to white flowers; hairy, lobed leaves; roundish, prickly fruit

White to Green

Orthilia secunda

Sidebells Wintergreen
Stem to 8 inches; green to cream, bell-shaped flowers in one-sided cluster; mountains

Pyrola picta

White-veined Wintergreen
Stem 4–10 inches; flowers nod, petals cream to greenish-white; white-veined leaves; mountains

Phacelia hastata

Silverleaf Scorpionweed
Silver-hairy, 6–36 inches; flowers in tightly coiled cluster; veined leaves; widespread

Phacelia heterophylla

Varileaf Phacelia
Stems to 4 feet; clusters, curved, hairy; lower leaves lobed, upper unlobed; widespread

Trifolium repens

White Clover
Spreading, rooting stems 2–4 inches tall; spherical heads, tubular flowers; 3 leaflets; weedy

Xerophyllum tenax

Beargrass
Up to 6 feet tall with a dense flower cluster; grass-like leaves in thick basal clump; widespread

Ribes cereum

Wax Currant
Shrub; greenish-white to pinkish flowers; red to orange fruit; fan-shaped leaves; forests

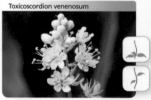
Toxicoscordion venenosum

Meadow Death Camas
Stem 6–18 inches; petals have yellow-green base; grass-like leaves; **toxic;** coast to mountains

White to Green

Actaea rubra

Baneberry

Clumps to 3 feet; clusters of tiny flowers; toothed leaflets; red or white fruit; **toxic**; forests

Holodiscus discolor

Oceanspray

Small tree; branching array with 10–100 small flowers; oval, toothed leaves; widespread

Sambucus racemosa

Red Elderberry

Small tree; domed flower clusters; fruit red or black; 5–7 lance-shaped leaflets; forests

Sambucus nigra

Blue Elderberry

Small tree; flat-topped flower clusters; blue-black fruit; 3–9 lance-shaped leaflets; forests

Prunus virginiana

Chokecherry

Small tree; cylindrical clusters; purple fruit; oblong, pointed, glossy, serrated leaves; forests

Valeriana sitchensis

Sitka Valerian

Stem 4–28 inches; dense flower cluster, stamens extended; lobed, toothed leaves; forest to alpine

Lithophragma tenellum

Slender Woodland Star

Stem 3–12 inches; petals white to pink with 5–7 pointed lobes; rounded, lobed leaves; sage to forests

Cardamine cordifolia

Large Mountain Bittercress

Stem 8–24 inches; dense clusters of 4-petaled flowers; rounded to heart-shaped leaves; mountains

White to Green

Noccaea fendleri

Wild Candytuft
Stem 2–12 inches; rounded cluster of 4 white to pinkish petals; clasping leaves; mountains

Claytonia lanceolata

Western Spring Beauty
Stem to 6 inches; 5 white to pink petals, often lined; lance-shaped leaves; sagebrush to alpine

Claytonia sibirica

Candy Flower
Stem 6–14 inches; white to pink, red striped notched petals; pointed oval, leaves; coast to forests

Oxalis oregana

Redwood Sorrel
Stemless; white to pinkish flower with reddish veining; 3 leaflets, maroon underneath; forests

Clematis ligusticifolia

Western Virgin's Bower
Vine; 4–5 hairy petals, showy stamens; fruit a silky plume; 5–15 lance-shaped leaflets; forests

Trautvetteria caroliniensis

False Bugbane
Stem 2–5 feet; clusters of 5+ flowers, showy stamens, no petals; deeply lobed leaves; mountains

Linanthus pungens

Granite Prickly Phlox
Stems to 16 inches; petals white to pale pink; crowded, prickly leaves; sagebrush to forests

Leptosiphon nuttallii

Nuttall's Phlox
Stems 4–8 inches; compact clusters, 5 petals, yellow throats; needle-like leaves; widespread

White to Green

Lloydia serotina

Alpine Lily
Flower stem 4–8 inches tall; 6 white petals with dark veins, yellow throat; grass-like leaves

Fragaria vesca

Wild Strawberry
Small white flowers and red berries; basal leaves with 3 leaflets with coarse teeth; forests

Glycyrrhiza lepidota

Wild Licorice
Leafy stems 1–4 feet; seed pods covered in hooked prickles; leaves with 13–19 leaflets; moist soil

Lupinus albicaulis

Sickle-keel Lupine
Stem 1–3 feet; spike of white, yellow, or purple flowers; leaves have 5–10 leaflets; dry forests

Lupinus arbustus

Spur Lupine
Stem 8–28 inches; white, blue, purple, pink flowers with a rear spur; 7–13 leaflets; sage to forests

Luetkea pectinata

Partridge Foot
Mat-forming; spike-like cluster; 5 petals around a yellow disk; narrow-lobed leaves; mountains

Goodyera oblongifolia

Rattlesnake Plantain Orchid
Stem lined with 10–48 small, white-greenish flowers; elliptic, white-streaked leaves; forests

Platanthera dilatata

White Bog Orchid
Stem to 3 feet; 2 side sepals, upper hood, drooping lip, club-shaped spur; lance-shaped leaves; wet soils

White to Green

Pedicularis racemosa

Sickletop Lousewort

Stem 8–20 inches; white to pink, upper is beak-like petals; lance-shaped, serrated leaves; forests

Monotropa uniflora

Indian Pipe

Slender white stems, 2–10 inches; bell-shaped, nodding flowers; scale-like, white leaves; forests

Heracleum maximum

Cow Parsnip

Up to 8 feet; umbrella-shaped clusters of small flowers; leaves with 3 pointed lobes; forests

Veratrum californicum

Corn Lily

Small flowers on branching stalks; tall corn-like stems; broad, strongly veined leaves; moist soils

Erigeron divergens

Spreading Fleabane

Branching stems to 16 inches; white to lavender rays; buds nod; narrow leaves; widespread

Erigeron philadelphicus

Philadelphia Fleabane

Leafy, hairy stems to 30 inches; flower heads with 150+ rays; clasping upper leaves; moist soils

Erigeron compositus

Cutleaf Daisy

Leafless stems, 4–10 inches; flower head hairy, rays white to bluish; leaves lobed; sagebrush to alpine

Lathyrus lanszwertii

Mountain Pea

Vining 1–3 feet; flowers white to purple, often with a red-lined upper petal; 4–20 narrow leaflets; forests

White to Green

Geranium richardsonii

Richardson's Geranium

Stem 8–32 inches; white to pink, purple-veined petals; leaves have toothed lobes; forests

Bellis perennis

English Daisy

Stem 1–10 inches; narrow, white to pinkish rays; oval leaves, surfaces hairy; coastal, weedy

Leucanthemum vulgare

Ox-eye Daisy

Stems 2 feet; leaves lobed or with blunt teeth; widespread, invasive to roadsides, meadows

Amelanchier alnifolia

Western Serviceberry

Small tree; clusters of 5–15 flowers; red fruit; oval, toothed leaves, blunt tips; widespread

Caltha leptosepala

Marsh Marigold

Stems to 1 foot; white petals, purple buds, many stamens; heart-shaped leaves; wet areas

Clintonia uniflora

Queen's Cup

Stem 6 inches; creamy flowers; blue berries; oblong, pointed leaves; mountain forests

Rubus parviflorus

Thimbleberry

Leafy thornless shrub 3–6 feet tall; edible red berries; lobed, maple-like leaves; forests

Rubus bifrons

Himalaya Blackberry

Leafy, thorny, sprawling to 16 feet; edible black berries; 3–5 pointed, toothed leaflets; weedy

White to Green

Cypripedium montanum

Mountain Lady's Slipper

Stem 10–28 inches; white pouch-like lower lip; brown upper petals; elliptic leaves; forests

Anemone occidentalis

Western Pasque Flower

Stems 6–24 inches; white to purplish-tinted petals; feathery seeds; narrow leaves; mountains

Cornus unalaschkensis

Western Bunchberry

Groundcover; diamond-shaped petals; fruit a cluster of red berries; elliptic leaves; forests

Erythronium montanum

Avalanche Lily

Stems 6–8 inches; flowers nod; pointed petals, yellow throat; oval, pointed leaves; mountains

Frasera speciosa

Monument Plant

Stalks 2–6 feet; whorls of purple-spotted green flowers; basal rosette of broad leaves; forests

Calystegia sepium

Hedge Morning Glory

Vine to 12 feet long; trumpet-shaped white to pinkish flowers; arrowhead shaped leaves; weedy

Oenothera pallida

Pale Evening Primrose

Stems 4–20 inches; buds nod, notched petals; narrow, toothed or lobed leaves; sandy soils

Trillium ovatum

Western Trillium

Stem 4–18 inches; 3 oval, pointed petals, fade to pink; 3 oval, pointed leaves; coast to forests

Streamside Bluebells

Stems 3–4 feet; fragrant, tubular, hanging flowers; elliptic, blue-green leaves; wet meadows

Silky Phacelia

Stem 6–16 inches; dense flower spike with extended stamens; hairy, fern-like leaves; meadows

Self-heal

Short spikes of small hooded flowers with a fringed lower lobe; elliptical leaves; forms colonies

Alpine Speedwell

Stems 4–10 inches; flowers clustered, 4 blue-violet petals; elliptic leaves; wet meadows

Hound's Tongue

Stem 2–4 feet; maroon to purple flowers with 5 rounded lobes; hairy, lance-shaped leaves; weedy

Hooked-spur Violet

Flower stem up to 4 inches; blue to violet petals; whitish throats have dark lines; forests

Freckled Milkvetch

Clumps to 3 feet wide; reddish stems; tubular, purple and white flowers; freckled pods

Slim Larkspur

Stem to 16 inches; loose flower spike, spreading petals, spur; wet sites, summer-blooming

Delphinium nuttallianum

Meadow Larkspur
Stem to 16 inches; dense flower spike, spreading petals, spur; dry sites, spring-blooming

Gilia capitata

Bluehead Gilia
Dense, rounded clusters; 5 petals and extended stamens; fern-like leaves; coast to forests

Lupinus argenteus

Silvery Lupine
Up to 4 feet; silver-hairy flowers with swollen, pointed base; 5–10 leaflets; sagebrush to forests

Lupinus polyphyllus

Large-leaf Lupine
Hairless stems to 5 feet; blue, lavender, or purple flowers; 5–17 leaflets; wet soil

Lupinus latifolius

Broadleaf Lupine
Stems 1–6 feet tall; blue to purple flower with white upper parch; 5–11 leaflets; forests

Lupinus lepidus

Elegant Lupine
Matted or erect, hairy stems; blue, purple, or white flowers; 5–9 hairy leaflets; woodlands

Medicago sativa

Alfalfa
Branching stem 8–30 inches; compact spike of blue to violet, pea-like flowers; 3 narrow leaflets

Sisyrinchium bellum

Western Blue-eyed Grass
Clumps 12–16 inches; 6 pointed petals, yellow throat; grass-like leaves; sagebrush to forests

Cichorium intybus

Chicory

Stems to 6 feet; light blue petals with 5 tiny points, darker anthers; common roadside weed

Campanula rotundifolia

Harebell

Stems 4–24 inches; bell-shaped, nodding flowers; 5 petals, pointed, spreading; narrow leaves

Polemonium pulcherrimum

Showy Jacob's Ladder

Stems 4–8 inches; pale-blue to purple flowers, yellow throat; 9–22 oval leaflets; mountains

Penstemon procerus

Small-flowered Penstemon

Stem to 15 inches; dense whorls of blue-purplish flowers; narrow, toothless leaves; forests

Penstemon serrulatus

Cascade Penstemon

Stem 1–2 feet; a single cluster of blue to purple flowers; clasping, toothed leaves; wet soils

Vicia americana

American Vetch

Vining stems 1–3 feet; purple to lavender flowers; leaves have 8–16 leaflets and twining tendrils

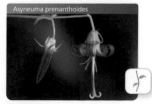

Asyneuma prenanthoides

Nodding Harebell

Stems to 30 inches; blue, dangling flowers, 5 petals curved back; long protruding stamen; forests

Dieteria canescens

Purple Aster

Bushy stems 1–4 feet; flower heads with 8–25 blue to purple rays, yellow disk; narrow leaves

Blue to Purple

Symphyotrichum spathulatum

Western Mountain Aster

Stems 1–2 feet; 15–40 narrow, violet rays; yellow disk; narrow, pointed leaves; forests

Linum lewisii

Blue Flax

Stems 6–36 inches; 5 petals with dark lines, yellow throat; narrow; pointed leaves hug stem

Erigeron glacialis

Wandering Fleabane

Up to 18 inches; blue, purple, or pink rays; lance-shaped leaves, smaller up the stem; meadows

Erigeron speciosus

Showy Fleabane

Stems 1–2 feet; many narrow ray flowers around yellow disk; even-sized leaves, hairless surface

Erigeron subtrinervis

Three-nerve Fleabane

Stems 1–2 feet; many narrow ray flowers around a yellow disk; even-sized leaves, hairy surface

Nemophila menziesii

Baby Blue Eyes

Stems to 12 inches; blue flowers, white center; leaves with 5–13 lobes along midrib; sage to forests

Gentiana affinis

Marsh Gentian

Stems 6–16 inches; tubular flowers; pointed petals, never open wide; narrow, pointed leaves; meadows

Clematis hirsutissima

Hairy Leatherflower

Stems 6–24 inches; nodding, hairy, urn-shaped flower, tips spreading; 7–13 narrow leaflets

Blue to Purple

Cardwell's Penstemon
Stems to 1 foot; purple to blue flower, hairy throat; elliptic, smooth to serrated leaves; forests

Penstemon cardwellii

Davidson's Penstemon
Mat-forming; tubular, blue to lavender flowers, white-woolly inside; oval leaves; mountains

Penstemon davidsonii

Crested-tongue Penstemon
Stem 4–16 inches; pale lavender to red-purple flower, streaked lips; narrow leaves; foothills

Penstemon eriantherus

Rydberg's Penstemon
Stems 8–24 inches; tubular blue to purple flowers in whorls, with gold hairs; moist meadows

Penstemon rydbergii

Common Camas
Stem 6–26 inches; conical cluster of 10–20 blue to violet flowers; broad, sword-like leaves

Camassia quamash

Columbian Monkshood
Stems 1–6 feet; flowers with hood-like upper petals; deeply lobed leaves; all parts **toxic**

Aconitum columbianum

Green-banded Mariposa Lily
Stem 8–20 inches; 3 hairy petals, striped green on the outside, purple banded inside; sage to forests

Calochortus macrocarpus

Western Blue Flag
Classic iris flowers, blue-streaked petals with yellow nectar guide; long, slender leaves; forests

Iris missouriensis

Adventure Quick Guides

Only Pacific Northwest Wildflowers

Organized by color for quick
and easy identification

Simple and convenient—narrow your choices by color and leaf attachment, and view just a few wildflowers at a time

- Pocket-size format—easier than laminated foldouts

- Professional photos of flowers in bloom

- Similar colors grouped together to ensure that you quickly find what you're looking for

- Leaf icons for comparison and identification

- Easy-to-use information for even casual observers

- Expert author is a skilled botanist and photographer

Get these *Adventure Quick Guides* for your area

ISBN 978-1-59193-827-9

9 781591 938279

5 0 9 9 5

$9.95

Adventure
PUBLICATIONS
an imprint of AdventureKEEN

NATURE/WILDFLOWERS/PACIFIC NW